© 2004 by Barbour Publishing, Inc.

ISBN 1-59310-002-7

Cover image © Digital Vision

Scripture quotations, unless otherwise noted, are taken from the King James Version of the Bible.

Scripture quotations marked NIV are taken from the HOLY BIBLE, NEW INTERNATIONAL VERSION®. NIV®. Copyright © 1973, 1978, 1984 by International Bible Society. Used by permission of Zondervan Publishing House. All rights reserved.

Published by Humble Creek, P.O. Box 719, Uhrichsville, Ohio 44683

Printed in China.
5 4 3 2 1

MOTHER'S *Love*

Wanda E. Brunstetter

HUMBLE CREEK
INSPIRATION FOR LIFE

MOTHER'S *Love*

There is something special and unique
about a mother's love for her child.
As a mother, it has always been my prayer that
my children and grandchildren would see the love
of God through His Spirit living in me.
God wants all mothers to receive the fruits of the Spirit,
which they can pass down as a gift of love to their children.

But the fruit of the Spirit is love, joy, peace, patience, kindness,
goodness, faithfulness, gentleness and self-control.

GALATIANS 5:22–23 NIV

CHAPTER 1

Love

Love is an image of God, and not a lifelong image, but the living essence of the divine nature which beams full of all goodness.

MARTIN LUTHER

It is a proven fact that all children need love. Without it, they will not thrive— emotionally, physically, or spiritually. A mother's love is unconditional and will touch a child's heart for years to come.

Love gives itself; it is not bought.

Henry Wadsworth Longfellow

Maternal love! thou word that sums all bliss.

Pollock

A baby is born all wrinkly and red,
But Mother looks beyond the wrinkles and loves instead.
A child might act mischievous or headstrong,
Yet Mother sees far beyond each little wrong.
A child needs love, unconditional and true,
A mother's love nurtures and instructs with wisdom too.

Wanda Brunstetter

This is my commandment,
That ye love one another,
as I have loved you.

JOHN 15:12

A FRIEND LOVETH AT ALL TIMES.

PROVERBS 17:17

Beloved, let us love one another: for love is of God;
and every one that loveth is born of God, and knoweth God.

1 JOHN 4:7

MOTHER'S Love

MOTHER'S *Love*

Make Me a Blessing

Give as 'twas given to you in your need;
Love as the Master loved you.
Be to the helpless a helper indeed;
Unto your mission be true.
Make me a blessing; make me a blessing.
Out of my life may Jesus shine.
Make me a blessing, O Savior, I pray.
Make me a blessing to someone today.

IRA B. WILSON

CHAPTER 2

Joy

When we speak of joy it is not something we are after, but something that will come to us when we are after God and duty.

HORACE BUSHNELL

Children learn by example,
and a mother's joy is contagious.
A happy child has a joyful mother.
A mother's joy comes from God.
Through a yielded spirit she finds
her joy in the Lord.

No joy in nature is so sublimely affecting as the joy of a mother at the good fortune of her child.

JEAN PAUL RICHTER

WE CAN DO NOTHING WELL
WITHOUT JOY,
AND A GOOD CONSCIENCE WHICH IS
THE GROUND OF JOY.

RICHARD SIBBES

Joy in this world is like a rainbow, which in the morning only appears in the west, or toward the evening sky; but in the latter hours of the day casts its triumphal arch over the east, or morning sky.

JEAN PAUL RICHTER

You have made known to me the path of life;
you will fill me with joy in your presence,
with eternal pleasures at your right hand.

PSALM 16:11 NIV

FOR THE JOY OF THE LORD
IS YOUR STRENGTH.

NEHEMIAH 8:10

Well done, good and faithful servant;
thou hast been faithful over a few things,
I will make thee ruler over many things:
enter thou into the joy of thy lord.

MATTHEW 25:23

MOTHER'S
Love

MOTHER'S *Love*

How Great Our Joy

This Gift of God we'll cherish well,
That ever joy our hearts shall fill.
How great our joy! Great our joy!
Joy, joy, joy! Joy, joy, joy!
Praise we the Lord in heaven on high!
Praise we the Lord in heaven on high!

TRADITIONAL GERMAN CAROL

CHAPTER 3

Peace

Peace is the evening star of the soul, as virtue is its sun; and the two are never far apart.

CHARLES CALEB COLTON

When a mother exudes a sense of peace
and tranquility, her family feels calm.
Peacefulness brings healing to a troubled spirit.
A peaceful mother is like a medicinal balm.
Peace and assurance of Mother's love are
necessary ingredients for a happy home.

Speak, move, act in peace, as if you were in prayer. In truth, this is prayer.

FRANÇOIS FÉNELON

PEACE IS SUCH A PRECIOUS JEWEL
THAT I WOULD GIVE ANYTHING FOR IT
BUT TRUTH.

MATTHEW HENRY

Children know when Mother is at peace,
Troubles and problems all seem to cease.
Mother's soft touch and gentle
    words of love,
Are like healing balm from
    heaven above.

WANDA BRUNSTETTER

THE LORD WILL GIVE STRENGTH
UNTO HIS PEOPLE;
THE LORD WILL BLESS HIS PEOPLE
WITH PEACE.

PSALM 29:11

Aim for perfection, listen to my appeal, be of one mind, live in
peace. And the God of love and peace will be with you.

2 CORINTHIANS 13:11 NIV

Let the peace of Christ rule in your hearts,
since as members of one body
you were called to peace.
And be thankful.

COLOSSIANS 3:15 NIV

MOTHER'S
Love

MOTHER'S *Love*

Constantly Abiding

There's a peace in my heart that the world never gave,
A peace it cannot take away.
Though the trials of life may surround like a cloud,
I've a peace that has come there to stay!

ANNE S. MURPHY

CHAPTER 4

Patience

Patient waiting is often the highest way of doing
God's will.

JEREMY COLLIER

It is often said that patience is a virtue.
It's also a reflection of a mother's love.
To be patient and long-suffering with one's family
is the true measure of love.
A mother's patience is
a fine example to her children.

There is one form of hope which is never unwise, and which certainly does not diminish with the increase of knowledge. In that form it changes its name, and we call it patience.

BULWER

Patience strengthens the spirit, sweetens the temper, stifles anger, extinguishes envy, subdues pride, bridles the tongue, restrains the hand, and tramples upon temptations.

BISHOP HORNE

A patient mother has happy children who grow strong in the knowledge of their mother's love.

But that on the good ground are they,
which in an honest and good heart,
having heard the word, keep it,
and bring forth fruit with patience.

LUKE 8:15

KNOWING THIS,
THAT THE TRYING OF YOUR FAITH
WORKETH PATIENCE.

JAMES 1:3

For ye have need of patience, that,
after ye have done the will of God,
ye might receive the promise.

HEBREWS 10:36

MOTHER'S
Love

Love

O Master,
Let Me Walk with Thee

Teach me thy patience! still with Thee
In closer, dearer company,
In work that keeps faith sweet and strong,
In trust that triumphs over wrong.

WASHINGTON GLADDEN

CHAPTER 5

Kindness

A kind heart is a fountain of gladness,
making everything in its vicinity freshen into smiles.

WASHINGTON IRVING

Kindness and love go hand in hand.
A mother's kindness is reflected in her love.
If a mother shows kindness to her children,
they will learn to be kind and loving to others.
A mother's kindness is a gift to her family.

I expect to pass through life but once. If, therefore, there be any kindness I can show, or any good thing I can do to any fellow being, let me do it now, and not defer or neglect it, as I shall not pass this way again.

WILLIAM PENN

Kindness in women, not their beauteous looks,
shall win my love.

WILLIAM SHAKESPEARE

A mother's kindness goes a long way,
A mother's kindness brightens her children's day.
A mother's kindness is a way of
    showing love,
A mother's kindness is gentle as
    a dove.

WANDA BRUNSTETTER

Therefore, as God's chosen people, holy and dearly loved,
clothe yourselves with compassion, kindness,
humility, gentleness and patience.

COLOSSIANS 3:12 NIV

AND TO GODLINESS BROTHERLY KINDNESS;
AND TO BROTHERLY KINDNESS CHARITY.

2 PETER 1:7

Love is patient, love is kind.
It does not envy,
it does not boast,
it is not proud.

1 CORINTHIANS 13:4 NIV

MOTHER'S Love

O to Be Like Thee

O to be like Thee, full of compassion,
Loving, forgiving, tender, and kind,
Helping the helpless,
Cheering the fainting,
Seeking the wandering sinner to find.
O to be like Thee! O to be like Thee,
Blessed Redeemer, pure as Thou art!
Come in Thy sweetness; come in Thy fullness;
Stamp Thine own image deep on my heart.

THOMAS O. CHISHOLM

CHAPTER 6

Goodness

To be good, we must do good; and by doing good we take a sure means of being good, as the use and exercise of our muscles increase their power.

TRYON EDWARDS

The dictionary defines goodness as
"excellence or virtue."
A mother's love may be seen through
her goodness and moral excellence.
Setting a good example for her children is
one of the best ways a mother can show love.

He who loves goodness harbors angels,
reveres reverence, and lives with God.

RALPH WALDO EMERSON

Goodness consists not in
the outward things we do,
but in the inward thing we are.
To be good is the great thing.

E. H. CHAPIN

We must first be made good, before we can do good;
we must first be made just,
before our works can please God—
for when we are justified by faith
in Christ, then come good works.

LEWIS LATIMER

Heaviness in the heart of man maketh it stoop:
but a good word maketh it glad.

PROVERBS 12:25

PROVE ALL THINGS;
HOLD FAST THAT WHICH IS GOOD.

1 THESSALONIANS 5:21

"And I will teach you
the way that is good and right."

1 SAMUEL 12:23 NIV

MOTHER'S *Love*

MOTHER'S *Love*

Let the Beauty of Jesus Be Seen in Me

Let the beauty of Jesus be seen in me—
All His wonderful passion and purity!
O Thou Spirit divine,
All my nature refine,
'Til the beauty of Jesus be seen in me.

ALBERT ORSBORN

CHAPTER 7

Faithfulness

Faith makes the discords of the present
the harmonies of the future.

ROBERT COLLYER

A faithful mother is true to her beliefs
in God as well as her family.
By her example a faithful mother teaches her children
to have faith and become true to their word.
A faithful mother is a loving mother.

Christian faith is a grand cathedral,
with divinely pictured windows.
Standing without, you can see no glory,
nor can imagine any, but standing
within, every ray of light reveals a
harmony of unspeakable splendors.

NATHANIEL HAWTHORNE

A mother's faith gives hope to her child,
Stability and trust in a world gone wild.
A mother's faith is handed down,
In the next generation it will be found.
A mother's faith is steadfast and sure,
Her children desire to be like her.

WANDA BRUNSTETTER

It is good to praise the LORD and make music
to your name, O Most High, to proclaim your love
in the morning and your faithfulness at night.

PSALM 92:1–2 NIV

BELOVED,
THOU DOEST FAITHFULLY WHATSOEVER
THOU DOEST TO THE BRETHREN,
AND TO STRANGERS.

3 JOHN 5

The only thing that counts is
faith expressing itself through love.

GALATIANS 5:6 NIV

MOTHER'S
Love

O for a Faith That Will Not Shrink

O for a faith that will not shrink,
Though pressed by every foe,
That will not tremble on the brink
Of any earthly woe!
Lord, give us such a faith as this;
And then, whate'er may come,
We'll taste, e'en here, the hallowed bliss
Of an eternal home.

WILLIAM H. BATHURST

CHAPTER 8

Gentleness

We are indebted to Christianity for gentleness, especially toward women.

CHARLES SIMMONS

A gentle spirit has a calming
effect on all those around.
A mother's gentle words can have
a profound influence on her children's lives.
A mother's love is shown through her gentle words—
even words given in discipline.

Nothing is so strong as gentleness;
nothing so gentle as real strength.

St. Francis de Sales

IT IS EVERYTHING INCLUDED IN THE
MATCHLESS GRACE, "THE GENTLENESS
OF CHRIST."

J. Hamilton

True gentleness is founded on a sense of what we owe
Him who made us, and to the common nature which we
all share. It arises from reflection on our own failings and
wants, and from just views of the
condition and duty of men. It is
native feeling heightened and
improved by principle.

Hugh Blair

Thou hast also given me the shield of thy salvation:
and thy gentleness hath made me great.

2 Samuel 22:36

And the servant of the Lord must not strive; but be gentle unto all men, apt to teach, patient.

2 Timothy 2:24

But the wisdom that is from above is first pure, then peaceable, gentle, and easy to be entreated, full of mercy and good fruits, without partiality, and without hypocrisy.

James 3:17

MOTHER'S Love

Stepping in the Light

Walking in footsteps of gentle forbearance,
Footsteps of faithfulness, mercy, and love;
Looking to Him for the grace freely promised,
Happy, how happy, our journey above!
How beautiful to walk in the steps of the Savior,
Stepping in the light, stepping in the light!
How beautiful to walk in the steps of the Savior,
Led in paths of light!

ELIZA E. HEWITT

CHAPTER 9

Self-Control

If you would learn self-mastery, begin by yielding
yourself to the One Great Master.

J. F. LOBSTEIN

The spirit of self-control must be learned.
A mother who shows self-control to her family
will have children who grow up to be calm
and able to control their own emotions.

Every temptation that is resisted, every noble aspiration that is encouraged, every sinful thought that is repressed, every bitter word that is withheld, adds its little item to the impetus of that great movement which is bearing humanity onward toward a richer life and higher character.

JOHN FISKE

THOSE WHO CAN COMMAND
THEMSELVES, COMMAND OTHERS.

WILLIAM HAZLITT

More dear in the sight of God and His angels than any other conquest is the conquest of self.

A. P. STANLEY

But since we belong to the day, let us be self-controlled,
putting on faith and love as a breastplate,
and the hope of salvation as a helmet.

1 THESSALONIANS 5:8 NIV

For this very reason,
make every effort to add to your faith goodness;
and to goodness, knowledge;
and to knowledge, self-control;
and to self-control, perseverance;
and to perseverance, godliness.

2 PETER 1:5–6 NIV

MOTHER'S
Love

MOTHER'S *Love*

Take Time to Be Holy

Take time to be holy;
Be calm in thy soul—
Each thought and each motive
Beneath His control.
Thus led by His Spirit
To fountains of love,
Thou soon shall be fitted
For service above.

WILLIAM D. LONGSTAFF

And now these three remain: faith, hope and love. But the greatest of these is love.

1 CORINTHIANS 13:13 NIV